DEDICATION

Many thanks to my family and to all those who've
supported me on my life's journey and tolerated my
interpretation of humor. You know who you are.
Peace.

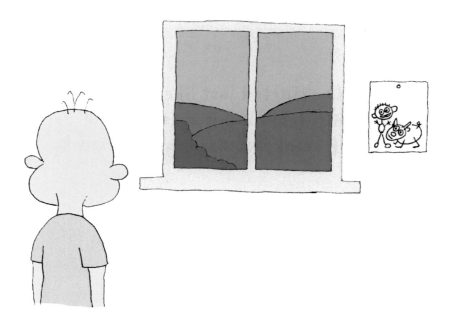

Why the tears? Elmo was lonely. You see, Elmo
lived on a farm where his mom and dad grew
vegetables. He was an only child – and since his
family lived way out in the country, he didn't
have any friends ... other than his imaginary
ones.

Elmo's mom and dad always worried that Elmo
spent too much time playing with himself.

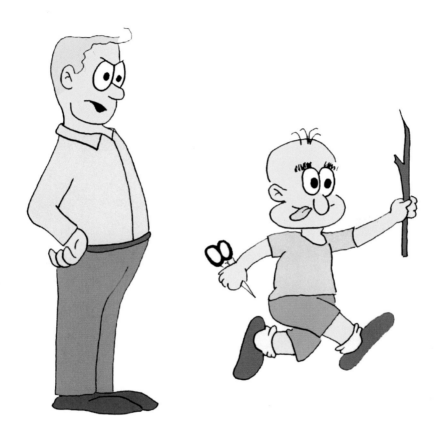

"That boy's gonna go blind if he's not more careful," Elmo's dad feared.

The nearest neighbor was more than a mile away. That neighbor, old Mr. Pickle, lived by himself and didn't have any children - or even a wife.

Mr. Pickle also lived on a farm. He raised chickens - lots of chickens that laid lots of eggs, which Mr. Pickle sold.

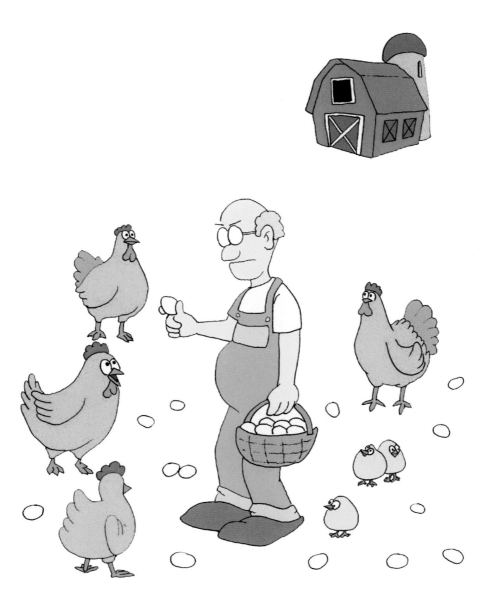

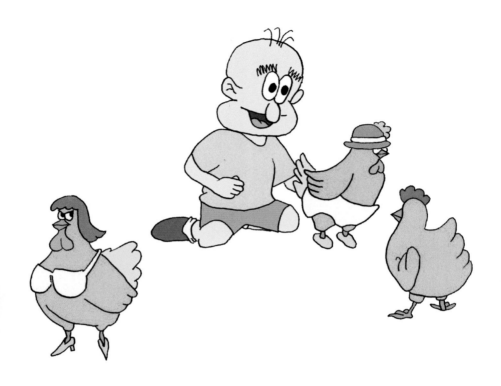

Elmo often spent several hours a
day playing with the chickens on
Mr. Pickle's farm.

Mr. Pickle was sad that Elmo seemed
so lonely.

"I got something for you, boy," Mr.
Pickle said one day.

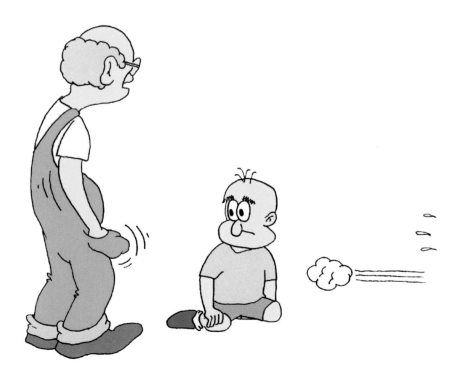

From his pocket, Mr. Pickle pulled out a key that unlocked a side door to his barn.

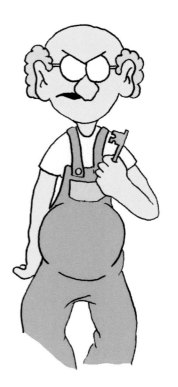

Mr. Pickle disappeared inside.

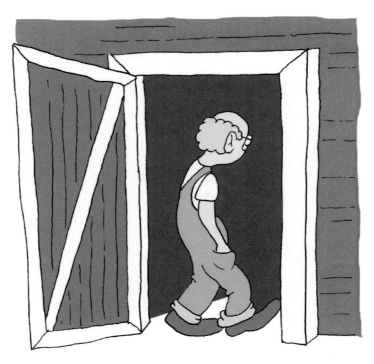

After a while, Elmo entered the barn and found Mr. Pickle standing near some hay bales.

"Whatchya doin', Mr. Pickle?" Elmo asked.

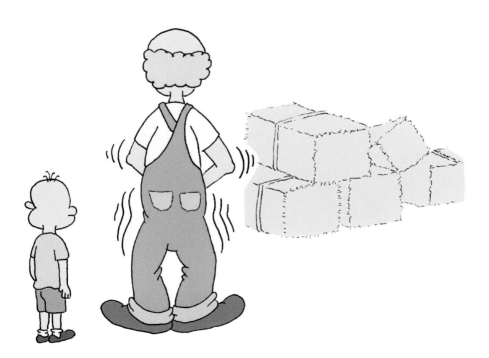

"Gimmee a minute, boy.
I wanna enjoy this. This
is gonna feel so good!"

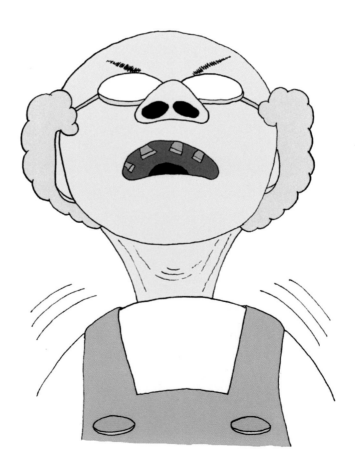

When Mr. Pickle turned
around, he surprised Elmo with
what was in his hands.

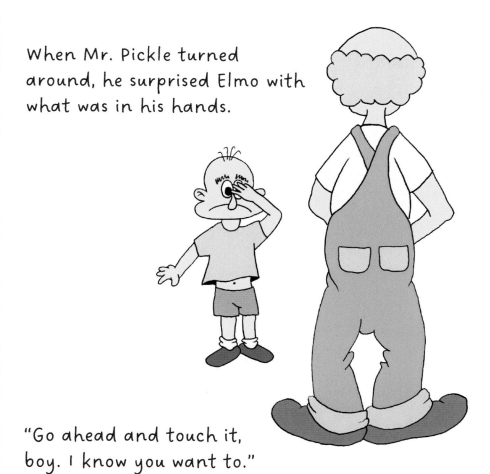

"Go ahead and touch it,
boy. I know you want to."

"What is it?" Elmo asked.

"It's a cock, boy. And if you think it's big now,
just wait. This here cock's gonna grow and grow
and grow!"

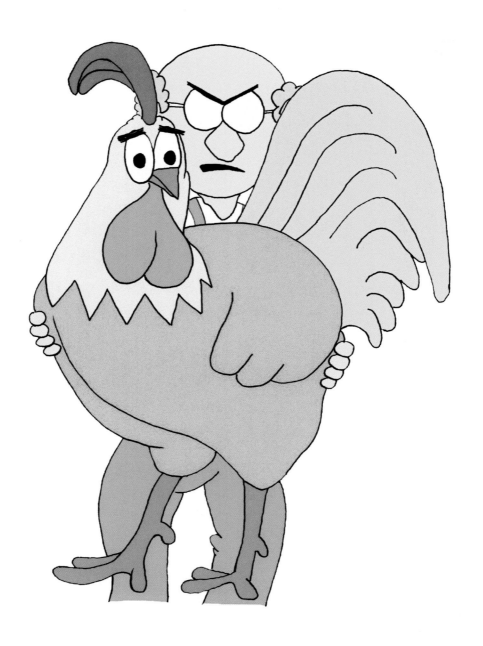

You see, that cock was a boy chicken ... and he was a lot different than the other chickens on the farm. For one thing, all the other chickens were girl chickens. And Mr. Pickle said boy chickens never produce eggs.

But the biggest difference wasn't his gender. Or his stiff comb or sagging waddle. Or his long, curving tail feathers. It wasn't even his propensity to scream whenever the sun peeked above an eastern hill on Mr. Pickle's farm. No, the biggest difference between that chicken and all the other young chickens was his size. He was five times the size of his sisters.

Suddenly, Mr. Pickle's cock lurched at Elmo, who stumbled backwards and tripped over a leather harness on the barn floor.

Mr. Pickle let go of his cock and
helped Elmo to his feet.

"I want you to take my cock, boy," Mr. Pickle said as he picked up the chicken. "Hold it with both hands. Cocks like it when you hold 'em firm. Not too tight. A little more tight. That's it. That's it!!"

"Oh gawd!!" Mr. Pickle exclaimed as a steady flow of thick, milky goo streamed from his cock onto Elmo's face.

"Looks like he done shit on ya, boy. You're gonna wanna wipe that off before your folks see it."

After Mr. Pickle helped Elmo clean up, he wheeled out a wagon that Elmo borrowed to bring his new friend home.

Elmo waved goodbye to Mr. Pickle as the elderly farmer disappeared back into the barn.

Elmo was so excited he could hardly contain himself. He stopped several times during the long walk home so he could play with his cock.

Hide and seek was one of the fun games they played. When Elmo would close his eyes, his cock would plunge head first into a thick bush lining the trail. Elmo's face contorted with excitement and anticipation as he fumbled around the prickly bush in search of his cock.

They passed several animals on the dusty trail, each a little leery of Elmo's enormous cock.

"There's a beaver," Elmo pointed out. "Maybe when you grow up, you'll be best friends!"

Elmo returned home just as his mom was putting supper on the kitchen table. When his mom saw the chicken, she shrieked ecstatically.

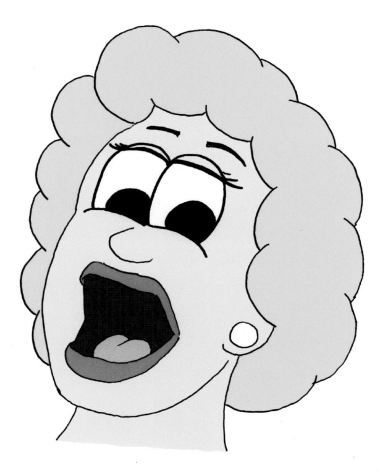

"That's the biggest cock I've ever seen!"

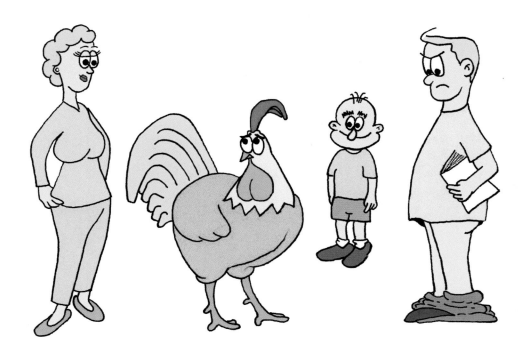

Elmo's dad was in the bathroom and hurried out to see what his wife was gushing on about. He was taken aback by how much his wife adored the cock. "I've seen bigger," he bristled. "In fact, when I was younger, I had a cock that was huge." Elmo's mom just rolled her eyes. "I'm sure you did," she mused. "I'm sorry I never saw it."

From that moment on, Elmo's dad seemed a little jealous of his young son's cock.

After supper, Elmo headed straight to his
room. Of course he couldn't keep his hands
off his cock. Lying on his bed, he played with
it for hours and didn't care if his cock soiled
the sheets. Elmo's cock thoroughly enjoyed
having its neck stroked. It felt so good and
was so soothing.

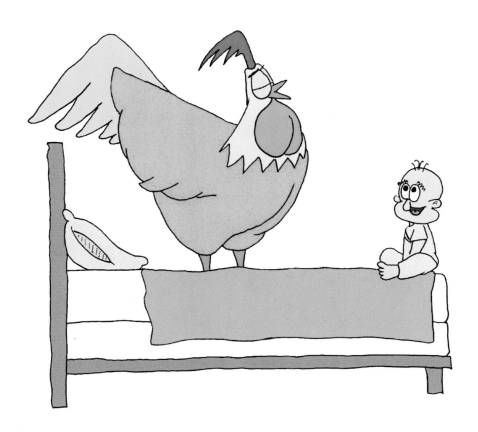

Eventually, Elmo grew exhausted
and drifted off to sleep.

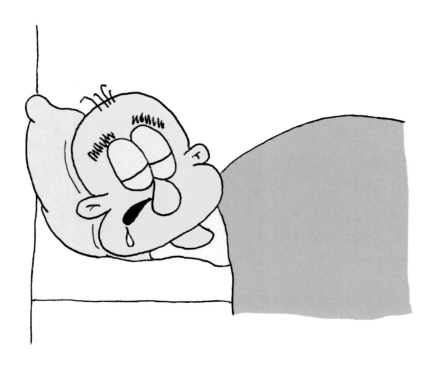

That night, Elmo dreamed about his cock. He dreamed that it was the biggest cock in the whole world. It was so big and crowed so loud that people miles away shuddered whenever his cock woke them up in the morning.

This was Elmo's best dream ever! He was rich ... and famous ... and very popular, especially with women.

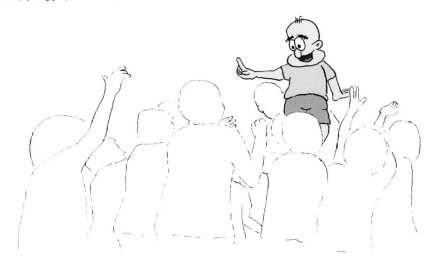

Just as his dream was coming to a climax ... COCK-A-DOODLE-DOO!! His eyes popped open as the sun peeked through his bedroom window. Sure enough, Elmo looked down to find that his cock was wide awake.

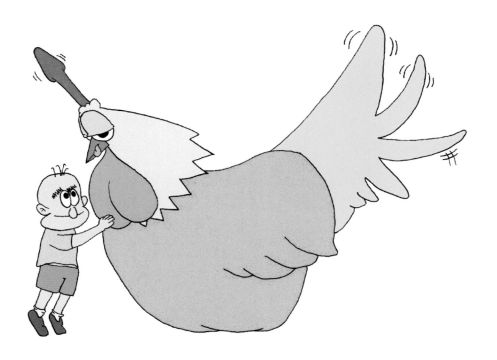

Elmo's cock seemed to grow every time that he or his mom touched it, which was often. They couldn't keep their hands off it!

About the only time Elmo let go of his cock was when he ate ... and only because his dad didn't want to see Elmo's cock at the table.

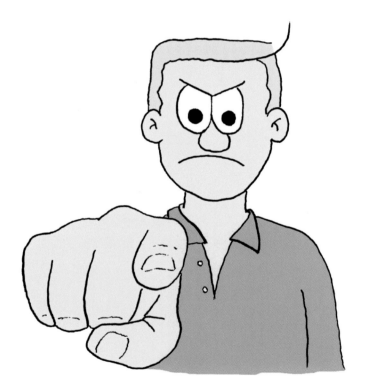

"Stop playing with your cock," he'd say. "It's time to eat."

Days turned into weeks, and weeks turned into months. And with every new turn of the calendar, Elmo's cock grew bigger and bigger. Word of Elmo's giant cock spread. The local newspaper even published a story on it. Elmo's cock was front-page news!

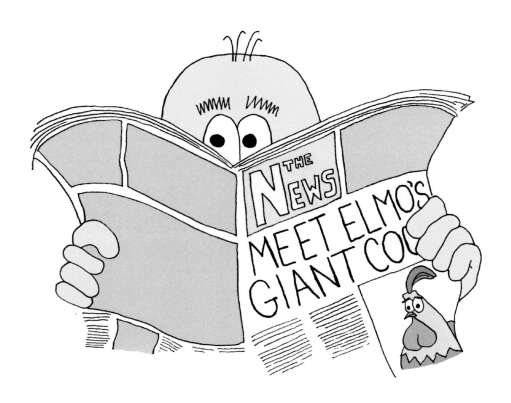

But not everyone thought bigger was better when it came to Elmo's cock. Like Dr. Stubbs, the local doctor. He thought Elmo's cock was too big.

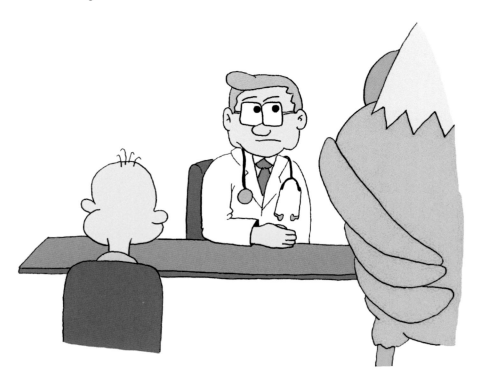

"It could become deformed," he warned. "If its blood flow becomes constricted, your cock could start to shrink."

And wouldn't you know it, but that's exactly what eventually happened.

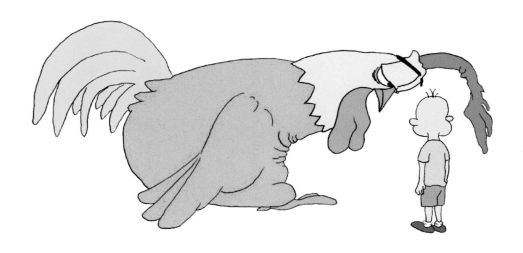

The arteries straining to pump blood throughout Elmo's giant cock began to atrophy. Within days, Elmo's giant cock was misshapen - its neck bent sharply to one side, and its once majestic head drooped.

Dr. Stubbs prescribed medicine - a blue pill that Elmo hoped would make his cock grow. But the pills only grew Elmo's cock for short periods of time. And after a while, the pills were totally ineffective.

A local inventor proposed building a pump that would be surgically implanted in Elmo's cock and controlled by an app on his phone.

"With a little digital manipulation, I'll make that cock of yours as big as ever," he promised.

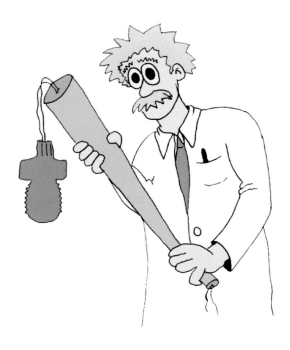

But Elmo was afraid of the operation and decided against it.

Meanwhile, Elmo's cock continued to shrink.

Naturally, Elmo's folks noticed what was happening to his cock and discussed their concerns when Elmo wasn't around.

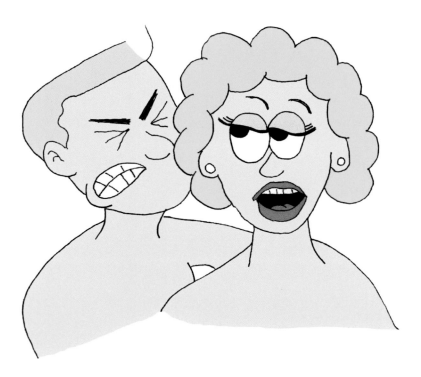

"I know you like a big cock," Elmo's dad whispered to his mom one night. "That big cock made you happy. You want that big cock, don't you?! Say it!!"

The next morning – for the first time since he brought the cock home – Elmo awoke before his cock did.

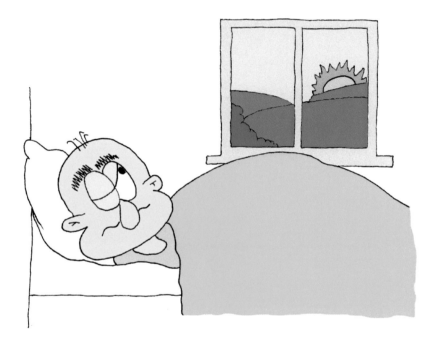

Fearing the worst, Elmo peeked under the covers and reached for his cock. It wasn't there. Elmo threw off the covers, but his cock was nowhere to be found.

Just then, Elmo noticed something moving on the floor, in the corner of his room. It was his cock, looking up with one eye trained on Elmo.

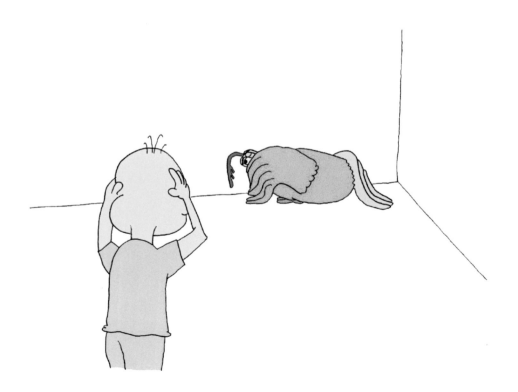

Elmo crouched beside the diminutive chicken as it shifted its weight from drumstick to drumstick.

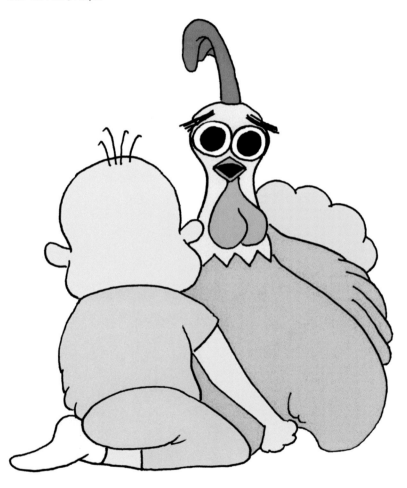

Instinctively, Elmo reached down and gently cupped his cock with both hands.

All worries quickly receded as Elmo made a startling discovery. With his cock cradled in one hand, Elmo felt two warm orbs in his other.

"What's this?!" Elmo whispered in disbelief as he discovered a pair of eggs on the underside of his cock.

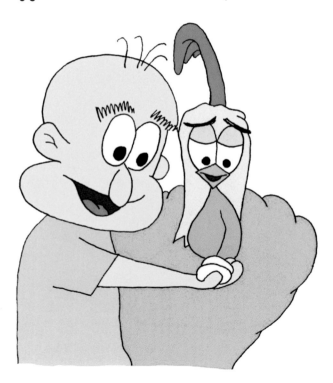

"Why ... you're not a cock at all!" he declared. "You're a hen!"

Right he was. Elmo's cock was no cock – it was just a masculine-looking hen with male tendencies and traits.

Elmo didn't care. He hugged his friend.

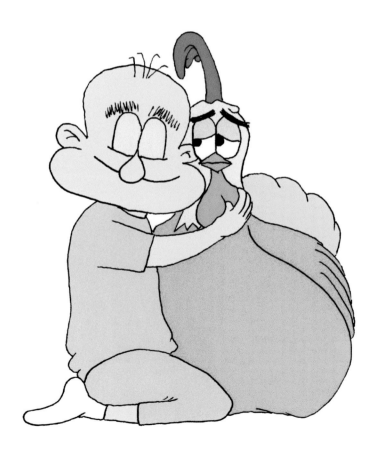

Just then, Elmo's dad entered the room and seemed unfazed by the revelation that Elmo's cock was actually a hen. He simply bent over and relieved Elmo of the two eggs.

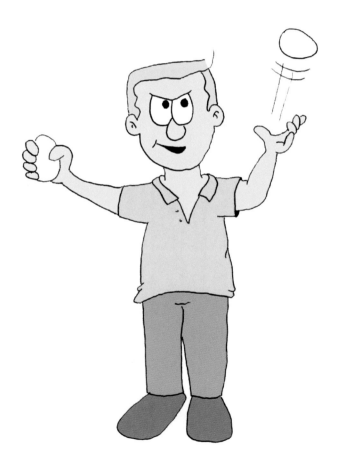

"Breakfast!" he proclaimed.

With a hot skillet sizzling in his ears,
tears again moistened Elmo's eyes.

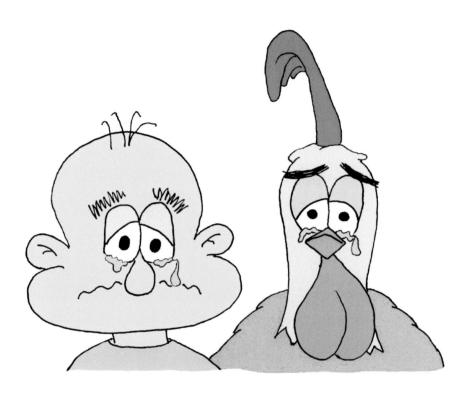

THE END

ABOUT THE AUTHOR

B.A. "Brian" Luscomb grew up in Southern California where he honed his humor and imagination by watching 3 Stooges reruns 'til his mom sent him outside to play. He inherited his funny bone from his dad — a creative genius and talented artist who introduced Brian to the works of Charles Schulz, Chic Young and Mort Walker. (Brian discovered Gary Larson and Bill Watterson on his own.) A journalism major in college, Brian toiled in the corporate world before jumping ship to draw and write stuff that didn't need management's input or approval. To see more of the sketchy and twisted things that Brian finds funny, check out his online cartoon, What_if_Cartoon.

Made in the USA
Las Vegas, NV
10 January 2024

84139419R00029